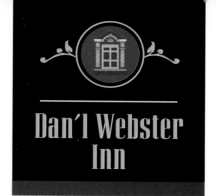

Dan'l Webster Inn

Dan'l Webster Inn

Sweet Potato Pie

2¼ cups sweet potato purée
3 eggs
⅓ cup brown sugar
¼ tsp. ground nutmeg
¾ tsp. ground cinnamon
½ tsp. allspice
¼ tsp. salt
1 tsp. lemon rind
1½ cups light cream
⅛ lb. butter, *melted*

Bake sweet potatoes, then peel and purée them. In a mixing bowl, mix all ingredients except butter and sweet potatoes. Mix sweet potato purée with egg and spice mixture. Add melted but cooled butter to mixture and mix until smooth. Pour into uncooked pie crust and bake until filling is set in middle of pie.

Basic Pie Dough

¾ lb. flour
½ tsp. salt
½ lb. cold butter
½ tsp. sugar
¼ cup ice water plus
1 Tbs. ice water

Mix the dry ingredients. Cut butter into dry ingredients to small pieces. Add water and mix just to form a ball, but do not overwork.

Macadamia & Cashew Striped Bass With Mango Sauce

Serves 4

1/3 cup unsalted macadamia nuts
1/3 cup unsalted cashews
3/4 cup fresh unseasoned bread crumbs
3/4 tsp. salt
    pinch of cayenne pepper
4 striped bass filets - 6 oz. each
1/2 cup flour
3 eggs, beaten
8 Tbs. unsalted butter (1 stick)
2 Tbs. vegetable oil
2 ripe mangoes
1/3 cup riesling wine
1 Tbs. fresh lemon juice
1/2 tsp. garlic, chopped
2 Tbs. honey

In a food processor, finely chop nuts, bread crumbs, salt and pepper. Dredge boneless, skinless filets in flour. Shake off excess flour, then dip into egg wash and bread crumb mixture. In a large sauté pan, sauté filets in 2 Tbs. butter and vegetable oil. Cook until brown on each side. Purée mangoes and set aside. In a small sauce pan, reduce wine with lemon juice and garlic until almost fully reduced. Add mango purée and honey. Season to taste with salt and pepper. Remove from heat and whip in butter. Serve filets drizzled with the warm mango sauce.

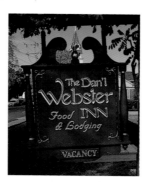

So much has changed in American society over the last three centuries. Where once stood a farmhouse is now likely the site of a high rise. What seemed ahead of its time then, is now termed archaic. America has certainly evolved, from ultraconservative to today's "these are the nineties" attitudes. In New England, one thing has been a mainstay from the colonial era - the warm and intimate hospitality of its country inns.

The Dan'l Webster Inn of Cape Cod is no exception. Far more than a place to stay the night, the inn is a place to experience the cordial hospitality and unique traditions of a bygone era. From the nightly turndown service - complete with little chocolates on the pillow - to the finely appointed furnishings, the historic inn exceeds even the greatest expectations.

The elegant yet comfortable gathering room is an ideal place to visit with friends, play a hand of cards or simply unwind. As meal hour nears, delectable aromas fill the inn as a tempting prelude to the classic American cuisine served in its three dining rooms. An award-winning wine cellar provides the perfect accompaniment to the meal.

Bedtime has never seemed so charming as it is here, with bed linens pulled back, a freshly fluffed pillow and stately reproduction furnishings all around.

Of course, the best known guest of the inn was none other than Daniel Webster, renowned defender of the United States Constitution. Every spring, the illustrious politician frequented the inn, which incidentally underwent numerous changes in ownership and appearance since its establishment in 1692. What began as a house later became a patriot meeting post, tavern, hotel and today, a first-class inn.

The Whitehall Inn

Chocolate Ganache

Combine:
- 2 cups heavy cream
- 2 Tbs. butter
- 2 Tbs. sugar

Boil a few minutes. Remove from heat.
Add:
- 1 lb. dark semi-sweet chocolate
  good quality, chopped fine or grated

Spreading consistency should be that of room temperature butter.

Almond Judge Tarte

Frangipan:

Preheat oven to 325 degrees. Grease and flour a 10" cake or springform pan.

Cream together:
- 1 cup butter
- 2 tsp. sugar

Mix until smooth and combine with above:
- 1 lb. almond paste
- 1 egg

Sift, add to above:
- 1 cup + 2 Tbs. pastry flour
- 1 cup hi-gluten (bread) flour

Add, 1 at a time:
- 4 eggs

Add:
- ½ tsp. orange extract
- ½ tsp. almond extract

Pour into pan. Bake 20 to 30 minutes or until firm. Cool; refrigerate 2 hours.

Simple Syrup

Combine:
- 2 cups water
- 2 cups sugar

Boil for 5 minutes. Cool.

To assemble tarte you will need:
- 10" or 12" cardboard circle
- Frangipan, *cut into thirds*
- Fudgecake, *cut into thirds*
- Ganache
- Simple Syrup
- Raspberry (seedless) jam or apricot jam

On cardboard circle, alternate layers of frangipan, ganache, fudgecake and jam, moistening cakes with simple syrup as you go, until the last layer of cake is on top. Spread ganache on sides and top of tarte in a thin layer. Refrigerate 2 hours. Spread another layer of ganache on top and sides of tarte. Zigzag a decorating comb across top of cake to make a design. Refrigerate 2 hours or overnight.

Butternut Apple Bisque
Serves 10

- 5 lbs. butternut squash, *cooked*
- 3 lbs. apples, *peeled and chopped*
- 1 qt. apple juice
- ⅓ cup roux
- ½ cup brown sugar
- 1 qt. cream

Wash butternut squash and add ⅓ cup roux, mix well. Cook apples in juice and blend with squash. Add all ingredients and simmer. Thin with half and half to desired consistency.

Chicken St. Millay
Serves 1

- skinless chicken breast
- 1 cup mushrooms, *sliced*
- 1 Tbs. shallots, *chopped*
- 2 oz. white wine
- 1 tsp. lemon juice
- 2 oz. cream

Salt and pepper chicken, dust with flour. Sauté in clarified butter and shallots; brown one side, turn over, add mushrooms, lemon, wine, cream. Simmer until done. Remove chicken, reduce sauce. Top before serving.

Devil Fudge Cake

Preheat oven to 375 degrees. Grease and flour a 10" cake or springform pan.

Stir together:
- ¼ cup cake flour
- ½ cup + 1 Tbs. cocoa powder
- 1¼ cups sugar
- 1 tsp. salt
- 2 tsp. baking powder
- pinch of cinnamon
- ¼ tsp. baking soda

Add in and mix until smooth:
- ⅓ cup + 2 tsp. shortening

Add:
- ⅓ cup skim milk

Scrape bowl, mix until smooth. Then combine together:
- ½ cup skim milk
- 2 eggs

Add into batter in thirds; mix well, scraping sides of bowl. Pour batter into pan. Bake 30 to 40 minutes or until firm. Test with toothpick. Cool; refrigerate 2 hours.

L IKE a marriage made in heaven, it is often said that the seacoast town of Camden, Maine, and the lovely Whitehall Inn are perfect companions. An understated elegance and stately presence envelope the grounds of this inn, which holds a coveted place on the National Register of Historic Places.

Nearly a century ago, a sea captain's wife opened her home to guests, and the inn's premise of treating visitors to fine food and hospitable accommodations was born. Today, the inn's keepers take enormous pride in providing every comfort one might expect, for a stay at Whitehall has unique meaning to each guest. For some it means sipping lemonade on the terrace or whiling away the afternoon in a cozy rocker. For others it may entail a day of browsing through village antique shops or a brisk walk on the seashore. At day's end, a sumptuous meal of homemade soups, seafood specialties, fresh salads and enticing desserts awaits. After a good night's rest in a charming spool bed, one awakes to the aromas of warm baked breads, a telltale sign that this will be another good day at the inn.

Red Hill Inn

Broiled Rack of Lamb Topped with Feta Cheese Stuffing
Serves 2

4   oz. Feta Cheese
2   cups fresh bread crumbs, *shredded*
1   tsp. garlic, *crushed*
1   Tbs. Dijon mustard
    chopped parsley and melted butter
    (to make moist)
1   Tbs. tarragon leaves

Mix the above ingredients and bake in oven at 425 degrees until brown (about 15 minutes). Cut and serve with mint jelly.

Old Fashioned Vinegar Pie

1   cup butter, *softened*
2½   cups sugar
6   eggs
¼   cup vinegar
2   Tbs. vanilla extract
1   unbaked 9" pie shell

Cream butter in mixer bowl until light. Add sugar, beating until fluffy. Beat in eggs 1 at a time. Add vinegar and vanilla. Spoon into pie shell. Bake at 350 degrees for 45 minutes.

I F it has been some time since you last shared a candlelight meal or a romantic stroll along a garden path, a visit to Red Hill Inn of Center Harbor, New Hampshire is long overdue. The turn-of-the-century inn has been lovingly restored and now serves as a soul-soothing respite from everyday life.

Somehow the cares of the world seem to slip away, if only for a while, as you settle in for your stay here. The Southern-inspired mansion sets high above the shores of Squam Lake, whose pristine waters are ideal for swimming, boating and fishing. If spending the day indoors seems more appealing, the wide hallways, airy rooms, oversized windows and classic architecture offer a comfortable atmosphere for curling up with a good read or chatting with a friend.

Originally commissioned around 1900 by real estate developer Leonard Tufts, the impressive brick structure was built on Overlook Hill, a spot that affords a breathtaking view of Squam Lake and the majestic White Mountains. Upon completion in 1904, the mansion was christened "Keewaydin" for the strong northerly winds that sweep Overlook Hill. Over time, Tufts purchased nearby farms and homesteads, thus expanding the estate to include farms, kennels, sugar houses and orchards that spread over thousands of acres.

The Tufts family fell on hard times during the Depression and the estate was sold. The next three decades brought many owners, including European royalty fleeing Nazi Germany and the Belknap College. Eleven years of vacancy followed, during which the mansion fell prey to the elements and vandals.

The current proprietors took over in 1985 and carefully restored the mansion to its original glory. In addition to the interior, the grounds are delightful as well. A quaint little path fringed in fragrant herbs brings enjoyment to all who wander past. The thyme, rosemary, winter savory, and other herbs grown here enhance the delectable dishes served at Red Hill Inn.

Ten Acres Lodge

Seared Tuna with Enoki Mushrooms, Shiitakes, Port Cream Sauce and Wasabi
Serves 4

1	lb. "sashimi" quality centercut tuna
1	package Enoki mushrooms
6	large Shiitake mushroom caps
½	cup red wine
½	cup port
2	cups cream
2	Tbs. shallots, *chopped*
3	Tbs. wasabi powder
	salt and pepper, *to taste*
	assorted julienned vegetables

Carefully clean tuna of any tendons and sear briefly on each side in a heavy sauté pan. No oil is needed. Immediately refrigerate tuna. Reduce wine and port with shallots to syrup consistency. Add cream and strain. Season to taste with salt and pepper. Keep at room temperature to serve. Slowly add a small amount of water to wasabi powder and form a thick paste. Blanche and shock vegetables in ice water. Neatly slice shiitake caps. On a chilled plate, pour several Tbs. of port sauce. Slice tuna very thinly and fan 3 slices on each plate. Garnish with mushrooms, vegetables and wasabi paste.

Head Chef: Eric Bauer
Sous Chef: Heather Rasmussen

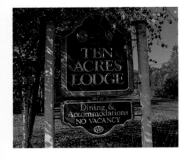

Grilled Marinated Vermont Partridge with Cherries, Morels and Cassis

Marinade:

½	cup red wine
½	cup red wine vinegar
½	cup olive oil
½	cup maple syrup
2	cloves garlic, *finely chopped*
½	tsp. juniper berries
½	tsp. black pepper, *crushed*
½	tsp. salt
2	each bay leaves
2	Tbs. whole grain mustard
	fresh thyme sprigs
6	partridge

In a mixing bowl, whip together wine, oil, maple syrup, mustard and salt and then add remaining ingredients. Partially debone partridge (leaving wing and leg bones in). Marinate for 6 to 8 hours, turning every few hours.

Sauce:

1	cup partridge or duck stock
½	cup demi-glace
2	oz. cassis
2	shallots, *chopped finely*
6	oz. morels
2	oz. dried cherries
	(Bing or Royal Anne varieties)
1	oz. Balsamic vinegar
1	oz. maple syrup
	salt and pepper, *to taste*

Bring cassis and shallots to a simmer. Add partridge stock and demi-glace, vinegar and maple syrup and bring to a simmer. Add cherries and morels and bring to a simmer again. Reduce to sauce consistency and season to taste with salt and pepper. Grill the birds over a moderate wood fired grill until done, or mark birds on the grill and finish them in a 440 degree oven, about 15 minutes. Birds should reach an internal temperature of 160 degrees to be safely eaten.

Chocolate "Turtle" Tart (Chocolate Pecan Caramel Tart)

Serves 16

Crust:
1¼ cups pecan pieces
⅓ cup sugar
Grind ingredients finely in food processor.

¼ cup unsalted butter, *melted*
Add to the above mixture. Press mixture firmly into 10" tart pan (with removable bottom) on the bottom and up the sides. Bake at 350 degrees until golden brown and nutty smelling, about 18 minutes. Cool on a rack.

Filling:
1¼ cups heavy cream
Simmered in a heavy sauce pan.
11 oz. semi-sweet chocolate
Chop finely.
Place in a large bowl and pour hot cream over chocolate. Whisk until chocolate is melted and mixture is smooth.
1½ cups toasted pecan pieces
Add to chocolate mixture, stir well.
Pour into cooled tart crust and chill.

Caramel Sauce:
½ cup unsalted butter
Melt in a large skillet.
1 cup sugar
Stir in and cook until light brown.
1 cup heavy cream
Add slowly, stirring on low heat until smooth. Strain to remove lumps.

To serve, place wedge of tart on plate and pour warm caramel sauce over the top. Garnish with a toasted pecan piece. Extra caramel sauce can be kept, covered in refrigerator for one month.

Pastry Chef: Holly Wilkins

Broiled Oysters "Ulrika" with Smoked Salmon, Dill and Caviar

5-6 oysters per person - *depending on size*
½ lb. butter, *softened*
2 oz. smoked salmon, *diced fine*
¼ cup dill, *chopped*
1 oz. white wine
½ oz. lemon juice
3 egg yolks
salt and pepper, *to taste*

Clean and scrub oysters, open and leave on the half shell. In a mixing bowl, whip together butter, wine, lemon juice and egg yolks. Fold in smoked salmon and dill. Season with salt and pepper to taste. Place two Tbs. of butter on each oyster and bake at 450 degrees for 10 minutes. Finish under a broiler until golden brown. Garnish with caviar and a dill sprig.

Head Chef: Eric Bauer
Sous Chef: Heather Rasmussen

A warm country ambience may be the first thing to note about Ten Acres Lodge. The stunning red lodge, trimmed in gleaming white, is perched on a hillside in lovely Stowe, Vermont. The main lodge, with its hand hewn beams and family antiques, makes an inviting first impression.

The lasting impression, however, is likely to come from the meals served at Ten Acres. Using only the freshest ingredients and a skillful hand, the chefs have mastered the lodge's signature dishes long-recognized as some of Vermont's finest. It is easy to see why the menu has won the accolades of both travel guests and genuine food aficionados. The difficult part is making a selection. Succulent venison steak? Roasted pheasant? Most definitely the apple spice cake with maple frosting.

Ten Acres is more than accommodating to those who want to do it all - or do nothing at all! For recreation, nearby attractions include Rock of Ages, Stowe Gondola and Alpine Slide, the renowned Stowe Ski Resort, hiking, canoeing, golfing and antiquing.

For a relaxing retreat, the guest rooms are individually appointed with comfortable furnishings and amenities. Spread a blanket beneath century-old maples and dream away the day. Or revel in the soothing hot tub overlooking majestic New England mountains.

Kennebunkport Inn

Bouillabaisse

This is a traditional Bouillabaisse broth with New England shellfish and fish. The flavor in the stock is from the mussels and clams rather than fish racks. It is served with rouille and toasted french bread.

$\frac{1}{2}$	cup good quality olive oil
2	Tbs. fennel seed
3	leeks, *coarsely chopped*
2	large onions, *coarsely chopped*
8	cloves unpeeled garlic, *cut in half*
4	stalks of celery, *chopped*
6	sprigs of parsley
10	whole black peppercorns
2	bay leaves
1	Tbs. dried rosemary
1	Tbs. dried thyme
$\frac{1}{2}$	cup tomato paste
1	can Italian plum tomatoes
$\frac{1}{2}$	orange rind, *grated*
	salt, *to taste*
2	lbs. mussels, *cleaned, not debearded*
1	lb. littleneck clams, *cleaned*
4	cups dry white wine
8	cups water
$\frac{1}{2}$	lb. swordfish
$\frac{1}{2}$	lb. halibut
4	lobster tails
8	jumbo shrimp
8	large sea scallops
16	littlenecks
160	mussels, *cleaned and debearded*

In large stock pot, over medium heat, sauté fennel seed in olive oil until fragrant, about 2 minutes. Add the next 4 ingredients and sauté until the vegetables are softened, about 10 minutes. Add the rest of the herbs and seasonings, top with mussels and clams, add wine and water. Cover and bring the stock to a boil, boil 10 minutes. Reduce heat and simmer for 45 minutes to an hour. The broth is done when it has reduced enough to coat the back of a wooden spoon. Strain the broth through a sieve, extracting as much of the vegetable juices by pressing down on them. Return stock to pot. Bring back to heat. Add the rest of the shellfish and fish. Cut the halibut and swordfish into small pieces. The fish is done when the clams and mussels are open.

Pumpkin Pie with Pecan-Brown Sugar Topping

This pumpkin pie recipe is a favorite of our baker, and is very popular with our guests.

Crust:

$1\frac{1}{2}$	cups all purpose flour
2	Tbs. sugar
$\frac{1}{4}$	tsp. salt
10	Tbs. chilled butter, *cut into pieces*
4	Tbs. ice water

Filling:

2	eggs
1	lb. pumpkin
$\frac{1}{2}$	cup sugar
$\frac{1}{2}$	cup brown sugar
1	tsp. salt
1	tsp. cinnamon
$\frac{1}{4}$	tsp. ground clove
$\frac{1}{4}$	tsp. nutmeg
$1\frac{2}{3}$	cups evaporated milk

Topping:

3	Tbs. butter
	chilled and cut in small pieces
$\frac{2}{3}$	cup brown sugar
$\frac{2}{3}$	cup pecans

For the crust: In a bowl of food processor, combine flour, sugar and salt. Add the butter and blend until mixture resembles coarse meal. Add the water, 1 tablespoon at a time until it begins to stick together. Gather the dough into a ball, flatten into a disk and chill for half an hour.

For the filling: Preheat oven to 425 degrees. In a bowl, combine all of the filling ingredients, mix well. Pour the filling into the uncooked pie shell. Cook for 20 minutes at 425 degrees, then turn the oven to 375 degrees and continue to cook 25 minutes. Add topping around the pie, leaving a circle in the middle. Bake for another 5 to 10 minutes.

For the topping: Combine all the ingredients in bowl of food processor. Pulse on and off until the nuts and butter are combined with sugar and lightly ground.

I N the vibrant coastal community of Kennebunkport, Maine, amid sandy beaches, rocky shorelines and tranquil harbors, sets the enchanting Kennebunkport Inn.

A lovely mix of old-world elegance and country charm shines through in everything, from the crisp awnings that adorn the porches to the friendly, yet impeccable service. Delicate lace curtains drape the windows and fragrant blooms fill the gardens in spring, summer and fall.

Breakfast, lunch and dinner are classic international fare. Favorites at the inn include an excellent bouillabaisse made with last-catch-of-the-day New England seafood and pumpkin pie topped with pecans and brown sugar, the inn's signature dessert.

English Trifle

Trifle is served on the dessert card every night. It is the signature dessert at the Inn. Other fruit can be used in place of strawberries (raspberries, bananas, kiwis, etc.).

1	12-cup glass bowl or trifle bowl
36	1½" macaroons
½	cup amaretto liqueur
1	12-oz. jar strawberry jam
1	12-oz. pound cake
⅔	cup cream sherry
6	pints fresh strawberries
	(or 4 10-oz. packages frozen berries, thawed and drained)
¼	cup toasted almonds, *crushed*
2	cups whipping cream
2	Tbs. sugar
½	tsp. vanilla
	Custard *(recipe at right)*

Custard:

18	egg yolks
¾	cup sugar
2¼	cups milk, *scalded*
1¼	cups whipping cream, *scalded*
¼	cup cornstarch, *dissolved in 6 Tbs. milk*
¼	tsp. fresh nutmeg, *grated*
1	tsp. vanilla

Beat egg yolks until thick and lemon colored. Blend in milk, whipping cream and cornstarch mixture. Pour into a double boiler and whisk constantly over heat until mixture thickens. Do not allow to boil. Remove from heat, add vanilla and nutmeg, cover with wax paper and allow to cool.

To Assemble: Brush flat sides of 15 macaroons with liqueur. Arrange flat sides up. Cover with strawberry jam, 1¼ cups custard and layer of pound cake soaked in sherry. Then cover the pound cake with jam, half the strawberries and another 1¼ cups custard. Repeat layering with pound cake, sherry, jam, berries, custard. Arrange remaining macaroons flat side down over the top and brush with sherry. Plastic wrap can be placed over the top at this point and kept up to two days. Before serving, whip cream with sugar and vanilla until stiff. Decorate top of trifle and whipped cream. A final garnish of almonds may be sprinkled over the top.

Rouille

½	cup bread crumbs *soaked in 1 cup water*
4	cloves of peeled garlic
½	Tbs. dried red pepper
¼	cup olive oil
2	drops Tabasco sauce
1	Tbs. paprika
3-4	spoonfuls of Bouillabaisse broth

Strain the bread crumbs and squeeze out extra moisture. In the work bowl of food processor, combine all ingredients except broth. Process a smooth paste and add broth gradually. You do not want the rouille to be too liquid. It should be the consistency of mayonnaise.

Longfellow's Wayside Inn

Roast Duckling
Serves 2

4½-5 lb. duckling
    orange slices
    orange sauce

Remove giblets and place duck breast side up on a rack in roasting pan. Place in preheated 350 degree oven and roast approximately 3 hours. You may baste, but it is not necessary. Remove duckling and let cool about 20 minutes. Remove back bone and split duckling lengthwise. Remove breast bones and place the 2 duck halves on baking pan. Before serving, put back in 400 degree oven for 10 minutes to crisp the skin. Serve on a platter and garnish with orange slices. Cover with orange sauce.

Orange Sauce

½   cup flour
½   stick butter or margarine
    or equivalent amount of chicken fat
2   Tbs. sugar
1   orange, cut in small sliced wedges
½   small can orange juice concentrate
1   pint of water or chicken stock
    (if water, add 2 bouillon cubes)

Melt sugar in 1 quart saucepan. Add orange juice concentrate, chicken stock and bring to a boil. Simmer 10 minutes, stirring occasionally with a wire whisk. In a 2-quart sauce pan, melt butter and add flour to make a roux. With wooden spoon, constantly stir over very low heat to remove starchy taste, taking care not to let roux scorch. Add stock to roux stirring constantly and allow to cook for about 10 minutes. Strain sauce and add orange wedges for garnish.

Delmonico Potatoes
Serves 8-10

6-8 large potatoes
     peeled, diced, cooked and drained
4   Tbs. butter
4   Tbs. flour
2   cups milk or cream
4   oz. sharp cheddar cheese, grated
1   small can red peppers or pimemtoes,
     diced and drained
     crumb topping

Melt butter in heavy sauce pan and add flour to make roux, mixing over low heat for 5 minutes. Be careful not to color the roux. Heat milk or cream in separate pot and add to roux. Let simmer for 10 minutes and whip in the grated cheddar cheese slowly. Mix potatoes with red pepper and place in greased casserole dish. Pour the cheese sauce over the potatoes and mix. Cover with crumb topping and bake in a preheated 350 degree oven for 45 minutes or until thoroughly browned. Serve hot.

Crumb Topping for Delmonicos

2   cups fresh bread crumbs
2   tsp. parmesan cheese, grated
2   tsp. paprika
2   tsp. salad oil
    salt and pepper, to taste

Place all ingredients in a mixing bowl and blend thoroughly.

Certainly times have changed since Henry Wadsworth Longfellow proclaimed: "As ancient is this Hostelry-As any in the land may be-Built in the old colonial day-When men lived in a grander way-With ampler hospitality." In keeping with his memories of the inn, today's proprietors of Longfellow's Wayside Inn take enormous pride in carrying on the congenial hospitality of centuries past.

The estate is sprawled over 106 acres of forest and farmland from which much of the inn's seasonal produce is cultivated. Ten generations of wayfarers have sought peace and tranquility at this historic inn of Sudbury, Massachusetts, now the oldest operating in America.

Eighteenth century law required innkeepers to provide for man, his horses and cattle. So when David How opened the inn in 1716 (known then as How's Tavern), he did just that by offering good food, restful accommodations and of course, shelter for animals.

Today, the fare remains classic New England, the guest rooms quite charming, and, of course, horses are still housed in the barn across from the inn.

pour in Jello mixture. Chill until set. Unmold on crisp lettuce cups and serve with cream dressing. To make the cream dressing, mix 2 cups whipped cream with $\frac{1}{2}$ cup sour cream, 1 Tbs. of pineapple juice and 1 tsp. of grenadine.

Cranberry Apple Crisp
Serves 10-12

2   cups whole cranberry sauce
$\frac{1}{2}$ cup sugar
8   apples, *peeled, cored and sliced*

Topping:
3   cups flour
1   cup sugar
8   oz. cold butter
2   tsp. cinnamon
1   Tbs. honey

Combine all topping ingredients and set aside. Mix cranberry sauce with sugar and bring to a boil over medium heat. Set aside to cool. Line bottom of a casserole dish with cranberry mix. Layer apples over cranberry sauce then spread topping over apples. Bake in a preheated 350 degree oven for approximately 45 minutes to an hour or until browned.

Minted Butter for Garden Peas

1   lb. whole butter
1   cup fresh mint, *chopped*
    salt and pepper, *to taste*

Melt butter and add mint, salt and pepper. Let simmer for 5 minutes and strain. Ladle desired amount of butter over cooked peas and serve hot.

Whipped Butternut Squash
Serves 10-15

5   lbs. butternut squash
    peeled, seeded and cooked
3   oz. brown sugar
3   oz. whole butter
2   Tbs. Vermont maple syrup
$\frac{1}{8}$ tsp. cinnamon
$\frac{1}{8}$ tsp. nutmeg
    salt and white pepper, *to taste*

When squash is cooked and drained, combine all ingredients in a mixing bowl and mix thoroughly. Taste and make any adjustments in seasoning.

Jerusha Peach Mold
Serves 12

12   ea. canned peach halves, *save juice*
$\frac{1}{2}$ cup cider vinegar
$\frac{3}{4}$ cup sugar
6   oz. orange flavored Jello
2   ea. cinnamon sticks
$\frac{1}{2}$ tsp. whole cloves

Combine vinegar, sugar, peach juice, spices and enough water to make 1 quart. Bring to a boil. Strain directly into mixing bowl with Jello mix and stir well until it becomes clear. Place peach halves in individual molds or custard dishes and

Old Lyme Inn

Fresh Curried Pumpkin and Apple Soup with Chicken and Apple Sausage
Serves 8

2   lbs. fresh pumpkin pulp
½   lb. onion, *sliced*
2   Tbs. butter plus 1 Tbs. butter
2   cups chicken broth
1   lb. apples, *diced and peeled*
4   Tbs. madras curry powder
1   cup apple cider or juice
½   lb. chicken and apple sausage
    cooked and cut into bite size pieces

In a 4-quart heavy pot on medium heat, sauté onions in 2 Tbs. butter until soft, add curry, sauté 2 minutes more, add cider, broth and pumpkin. Bring to boil, lower heat, and simmer ½ hour. Remove from heat, purée in food processor until smooth. Sauté apples in 1 Tbs. butter for 2 minutes. Add to puréed soup with sausage. Reheat and serve.

Chef: Stuart London

Raspberry Vinaigrette Salad Dressing

Blend well:
1 egg, ⅓ cup raspberry vinegar and 1 Tbs. whole grain mustard

Whip in slowly ¼ gallon olive oil.

Blend each of the following in individually:
⅓   cup raspberry vinegar
⅔   cup heavy cream

Season to taste with dill, salt and pepper. Enjoy!

Vegetable Flan

½   cup dried corn
½   cup milk
¾   cup half and half
1   Tbs. butter, *melted*
¼   tsp. basil & oregano
3   cups vegetables, *diced or chopped*
    (squashes, root veggies, onions, etc.)
¼   cup corn meal
¾   cup heavy cream
3   beaten eggs
1   tsp. salt and white pepper
¼   cup hard cheese, *grated*

Mix all ingredients together. Bake at 400 degrees for about 2 hours in a water bath. 9" square pan = 2 quarts. Enjoy!

Chef: Stuart London

Roast Rack of Venison with Cranberry Walnut Sauce
Serves 4-6

1   9-rib rack of venison or loin of venison
    seasoned with salt, pepper, thyme and rosemary
2   Tbs. clarified butter
1   large cast iron pan or Dutch oven

In a pan large enough to fit the venison, brown the meat off on high heat on all sides with the butter. When brown, put in a hot 400 degree oven for 12 minutes per pound. It should be cooked medium rare. Slice and serve with sauce (recipe on opposite page).

JUST past the ornate iron gates and lush terrace, the colonial-inspired Old Lyme Inn is a lasting tribute to an era of charm and elegance. Since its complete restoration in 1976, the inn is now idyllic of New England's fine colonial homes. From the well-appointed furnishings to the bannistered front porch, a visit here is like turning back the historical hands of time.

Built in the mid-1800's, the 300-acre estate served as a farm and private residence for one-hundred years. The turn of the century found the area's impressionist artists, brushes in hand, amid the beautiful meadows and woodlands behind the inn. Upon admiring the artworks displayed in the inn, it is easy to see why the glorious Connecticut landscape so inspired them.

Meals in the inn's Empire and Champlain rooms are reminiscent of the early days when fine linens, stemware and fresh flowers adorned the dining table. Careful and attentive service makes for a memorable experience. The fruits of the region - pumpkins, apples and cranberries - are amply used in the delectable dishes served here.

Chocolate Trinity Cake

The 3 layers are made separately, each using the basic cake layer recipe with a different chocolate: semi-sweet, milk, white. You will need 3 batches of the basic recipe.

Basic Cake Layer:

4   oz. ea. chocolate:
    semi-sweet, milk, white; *melt separately*
1   Tbs. Chambord liquor
½   cup sugar
⅓   cup plus 1 Tbs. soft butter
¼   tsp. baking powder
    salt
3   large eggs, *separated*
⅓   cup plus 1 Tbs. ground chestnuts
1   Tbs. plus ½ tsp. flour
*1 Tbs. dark cocoa powder - *used only in semi-sweet and milk chocolate layers*

Beat yolks with sugar 5 minutes until thick and light. Add Chambord liquor. Stir in melted chocolate. Stir in chestnuts and butter. Mix until smooth. Sift together flour, baking powder, and 1 Tbs. cocoa*. Gently stir into chocolate mixture. Whip whites with salt. Fold into chocolate mixture. Spread into 9" pan. Bake each layer at 400 degrees for 30 minutes or until firm. Cool 2 hours or overnight. Remove from pan.

Omit cocoa in white chocolate layer.

Filling:

8   oz. semi-sweet chocolate
    melted in large bowl
5   tsp. sweet butter
5   oz. heavy cream
5   tsp. raspberry jam
3   Tbs. Chambord liquor

Bring to a boil heavy cream, butter and sugar. Pour chocolate in. Stir well. Add Chambord liquor. Cool until consistency of frosting, about 2½ hours, stirring occasionally. Do not refrigerate.

Glaze:

8   oz. semi-sweet chocolate
8   oz. butter
3   Tbs. honey
    fresh raspberries, *for garnish*

Melt all ingredients together over double boiler. Stir until very smooth. Cool to the consistency of frosting, about 2¼ hours, stir occasionally. Do not refrigerate.

Assembly:

On a cake circle or serving dish, place the semi-sweet chocolate layer. Cover with half the filling. Place white chocolate layer on top. Cover with remaining filling. Place milk chocolate layer on top. Press down lightly. Spread glaze over sides and top of cake covering evenly. Place berries on top. Refrigerate until set. Serve at room temperature.

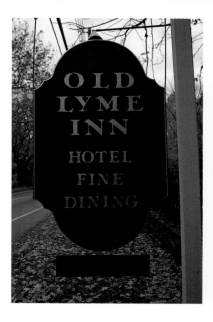

Cranberry Walnut Sauce

1   cup walnuts, *chopped*
½   cup game stock or strong chicken stock
½   cup maple syrup
1   Tbs. Dijon mustard
1   Tbs. walnut oil
¼   cup cranberry juice
1   cup fresh cranberries

Sauté walnuts in walnut oil until lightly browned in a 2 quart pot. Add the remaining ingredients, bring to a boil, reduce heat to simmer, reduce sauce by half. Serve over venison.

Chef: Stuart London

Skim fat from turkey pan juices. Strain, reserving juices and ¼ cup of fat. Heat turkey fat in saucepan. Add flour, cook over low heat 5 to 8 minutes until light golden, forming a roux. Add reserved turkey juice and stock to roux. Using wire whisk, whip until smooth. Add seasonings, simmer for 30 minutes. Strain, season with salt and pepper to taste. Add chopped giblets, if desired.

Bread Stuffing
(Yields 8-10 cups)

¾	cup butter
1	onion, *peeled and chopped*
½	bunch celery, *chopped*
¼	cup poultry seasoning
⅛	cup dried rubbed sage
4	whole bay leaves
1	Tbs. garlic powder
1	Tbs. dried rosemary
	dash of salt and pepper
2	tsp. dried thyme
3-4	cups turkey stock
20	slices day-old bread, *cubed*
	turkey livers *(optional)*

Preheat oven to 350 degrees. Butter two-quart ovenproof casserole dish. Melt ½ cup butter in large sauce pan. Add vegetables and seasonings, cook over medium heat until tender (5 minutes). Add stock, bring to a boil; boil gently (30 minutes). Taste for seasonings, add more salt and pepper if desired. Remove bay leaves. If you plan to use turkey livers, melt remaining ¼ cup butter in sauté pan. Add livers and sauté over medium heat until cooked through, (5 minutes). Drain off fat and chop livers fine. Place bread cubes and turkey livers (if desired) in large bowl. Add 2 cups stock with vegetables, mix well. Add remaining stock ½ cup at a time, just until bread is thoroughly moistened (amount of stock used will depend on how dry the bread is). Stuff body and neck cavity of turkey. Place remaining stuffing in prepared casserole, bake at 350 degrees (45 minutes) until golden brown on top.

Pan Gravy
Yields 2 cups

¼	cup flour
2	cups turkey or chicken stock
1	tsp. dried savory
1	tsp. dried rubbed sage
	salt and pepper, *to taste*
	turkey giblets, *cooked and chopped*
	(optional)

Red Lion Inn Apple Pie

5	pounds McIntosh apples
	peeled, cored, sliced (other tart apples, such as Cortland, may be substituted)
1	cup plus 1 Tbs. sugar
2	tsp. ground cinnamon
	crust for two-crust pie *(recipe below)*
1	Tbs. butter
1	egg
1	Tbs. milk

Preheat oven to 375 degrees. Place apples in large bowl. Combine 1 cup sugar and the cinnamon and add to apples, toss until well mixed. Fill unbaked pie shell with apple mixture and dot with butter. Fit top crust over filling and crimp top and bottom edges together to seal apples in. Whisk together the egg and milk. Brush top crust with egg wash and sprinkle with remaining 1 Tbs. sugar. Pierce top crust in several places with sharp knife. Bake at 375 degrees for 50 to 60 minutes or until the apples are tender when tested with thin knife. Yields 1 pie.

Pie Crust for Two-Crust Pie

½	cup cold butter
½	cup shortening
2¼	cups flour
¾	tsp. salt
½	cup cold milk

Blend butter and shortening together with wooden spoon in small bowl. Sift flour and salt together into large bowl. Cut in butter and shortening, using pastry blender or 2 knives, until mixture resembles cornmeal. Add cold milk, blend until absorbed. Divide dough in half, roll each half into ball. Wrap in plastic wrap, refrigerate until chilled, (30 minutes). (Or, if using a food processor, place butter, shortening, flour and salt in bowl; fit with steel blade. Process until mixture reaches consistency of cornmeal. With processor on, add milk slowly through funnel until dough forms ball.) When you are ready to bake pie, roll each half of chilled pie dough out on floured board until slightly larger than pie plate. Fit one half into pie plate, place filling inside, add top crust, flute edges together. Yields 2 crusts.

NORMAN Rockwell, consummate artist of true Americana, captured the spirit of what's been called the prettiest street in the land in his painting of Main Street, Stockbridge, Massachusetts. The friendly "hellos" from passersby and town buildings decked in holiday finery are still "the way" in this delightful town. The lovely Red Lion Inn, so stately and serene in Rockwell's painting, is very much the inn it appears to be.

A warm welcome has long been the hallmark of this inn, established in 1773 as a stopping place for stagecoaches traveling between Albany and Boston. With all that is new in the world today, to enter a place of such affable charm and elegance is a lovely change from everyday life. Sparkling Staffordshire china, colonial pewter and eighteenth century furniture are the furnishings of choice here. The view from the guest rooms is lovely, too, with the majestic Berkshires rising in the distance.

Guests at the Red Lion enjoy the goodness of traditional New England fare that has never gone out of style. Roast Turkey, Bread Stuffing, Pan Gravy and Apple Pie are mainstays of this kitchen and remain the tried-and-true favorites.

Roast Turkey Red Lion Inn
Serves 10

1	medium turkey, and neck, giblets, gizzard, heart, and liver(about 10 lbs.)
	Bread Stuffing (recipe on opposite page)
¼	cup butter or margarine
1	tsp. salt
¼	tsp. pepper
1	tsp. poultry seasoning
1	tsp. sage
	Pan Gravy (recipe on opposite page)

Preheat oven to 450 degrees. Remove neck, giblets, liver, etc. from turkey. Use liver in stuffing. Set rest aside. Rinse turkey cavity well, pat dry. Stuff turkey with Bread Stuffing, and truss opening. Place turkey on rack in roasting pan. Rub butter or margarine over skin. Combine seasonings and sprinkle over bird. Roast turkey for 10 minutes. Reduce heat to 350 degrees, roast for 20 to 25 minutes per pound, or until meat thermometer registers 185 degrees; this will take 3¾ to 4¼ hours. Baste often with pan juices. Meanwhile, if you like, cook all turkey parts, except livers for use later in pan gravy. In sauce pan, cook neck, giblets, heart and gizzard over low heat, in water to cover, for 2 hours until tender. Drain, remove meat from neck and chop all meats fine. Set aside to use in gravy. Remove turkey from oven and transfer to heated platter, reserving the pan juices. Let rest, covered with foil, for 30 minutes. Prepare gravy. Remove stuffing from turkey and place in serving dish, keeping warm until ready to use. Carve turkey and serve with stuffing and gravy.

Red Lion Inn Whipped Butternut Squash
Serves 10-12

3	pounds butternut squash, peeled, seeded and coarsely chopped
½	cup butter
¼	cup light brown sugar
2	Tbs. maple syrup
1	tsp. salt
½	tsp. white pepper
½	tsp. nutmeg
	fresh parsley, chopped

Preheat oven to 350 degrees. Butter a 3-quart baking dish. Boil squash in salted water to cover until tender, about 20 minutes, drain well. While still hot, combine squash with remaining ingredients (except parsley) in mixing bowl, whip with a beater until smooth. Taste and adjust the seasonings. Spoon squash into prepared baking dish, cover. Bake 10 to 15 minutes or until piping hot. Sprinkle with the chopped parsley and serve.

The Inn at Sunapee

All recipes by Susan Record Harriman

Chinese Spring Rolls
approx. 24

2   Tbs. dark soy sauce
2   Tbs. vegetable oil
2   Tbs. sesame oil
1   Tbs. minced ginger
1   Tbs. minced garlic
2   Tbs. oyster sauce
1   Tbs. Chinese vinegar
2   bunches green onion, *cut 1" length*
1   small Chinese cabbage, *thinly sliced*
6   oz. can water chestnuts, *sliced*
6   oz. can bamboo shoots, *sliced*
16 dried Chinese mushrooms
½   lb. bean sprouts
24 Filipino lumpia wrappers

Soak mushrooms for about ½ hour in hot water. Squeeze out moisture, cut stems and discard. Slice mushroom caps thinly. Lightly sauté ginger and garlic in vegetable and sesame oils for about 1 minute. Add green onions, mushrooms, water chestnuts and bamboo shoots. Sauté 2 to 3 minutes. Add soy sauce, vinegar, oyster sauce and cabbage. Sauté until cabbage is limp. Mix in bean sprouts and allow mixture to cool. Lumpia wrappers are round, so place about ¼ cup of mixture along one side. Roll over once to make a cigar shape and fold in both ends. Continue to roll to ½" of other side. Lightly brush exposed side with well beaten egg and finish rolling. Deep fry in vegetable oil at 350 degrees until golden (about 2 minutes on each side). Serve with a sweet and sour, plum or spicy dipping sauce.

Shrimp Santorini
serves 4

1½ lbs. large shrimp, *peeled and deveined*
4   plum tomatoes, *chopped*
3   Tbs. tomato paste
½   lb. feta cheese, *rinsed*
2   cloves garlic, *minced*
2-3 shallots, *thinly sliced*
¼   lb. mushrooms, *sliced*
1   tsp. fresh thyme, *chopped*
1   Tbs. fresh oregano, *chopped*
¼   cup brandy
1   cup white wine
3   Tbs. olive oil
1   Tbs. butter
    salt and pepper, *to taste*
    parmesan cheese, *grated*
    fresh parsley, *chopped*

Melt butter and olive oil in large, heavy fry pan. Add shrimp and cook until just beginning to turn pink. Add brandy to pan and flame. When flame subsides, add oregano, thyme, garlic and shallots and cook about 2 minutes. Remove shrimp with slotted spoon and set aside. To juices in fry pan add tomatoes and cook for 1 minute. Add tomato paste and white wine. When mixture begins to bubble, add feta cheese and mushrooms. Simmer until mixture is creamy. Return shrimp to pan and when hot, sprinkle with mixture of chopped parsley and grated parmesan cheese. Serve with linguini and a good, crusty bread.

W HEN the magnificent hues of autumn transform all of New Hampshire, and the crowds rush in to catch a glimpse of nature's spectacular show, perhaps the best place to be is The Inn at Sunappee. High above Sunapee Harbor and off the beaten track, this 1880's farmhouse is one of the area's best kept secrets.

Something about this place - be it the big wraparound porch or the hammered-tin ceilings - reminds one of simpler times. An impressive fieldstone fireplace heralds the old barn-turned-family lounge. It's a cozy spot to unwind or curl up with a treasured novel.

The innkeepers bring a lifetime of travels to their kitchen, where their innovative dishes are prepared with international flair and classic New England style. Asian travels may have inspired the Chinese Spring Rolls and Pork Singapore. The Venison Sausage and Indian Pudding, however, are classic New England specialties.

Linzertorte
(9 inch removable-rim pan)

Preheat oven to 400 degrees

1	cup sugar, *sifted*
¾	cup butter
1	tsp. lemon rind, *grated*
2	eggs
1½	cups raspberry preserve (*preferably seedless*)
1¼	cups all purpose flour
1	cup ground unblanched almonds
¾	tsp. cinnamon
¼	tsp. ground clove
¼	tsp. salt

Beat butter until soft and gradually add sugar, mixing until light and creamy. Beat in 1 egg at a time. Gradually add flour, almonds, cinnamon, clove and salt. Stir until completely blended. Chill dough ½ hour. Roll out dough slightly larger than pan and press onto bottom and sides of pan. Cover the bottom of the crust with the raspberry preserve. Cover top with "lattice" made from remaining dough. Bake 25 minutes or until golden brown. Remove torte from pan and serve with whipped cream.

Shelter Harbor Inn

Hazelnut Twille with Lemon Mousse Served with Raspberry Sauce and Mint
Serves 4

1   cup flour
1   cup sugar
1¼ cups hazelnuts
1   cup butter
1½ cups corn syrup
3   Tbs. dark corn syrup

Cream butter and dry ingredients. Add syrups and incorporate well. Scoop 1 oz. onto parchment paper and bake at 350 degrees for approximately 8 to 10 minutes. When baked, form warm shells over soup cup or bowl. Store in an airtight container.

Traditional Rhode Island Johnny Cake Recipe

1   cup water
¼   cup milk
¼   tsp. salt
½   tsp. sugar
1   cup Kenyon Johnny Cake meal
1   egg

Bring milk and water to a boil. Combine dry ingredients. Add liquid constantly stirring; add eggs and refrigerate. In a heavy skillet, spoon generous dollops of Johnny mix into hot bacon fat. Press and allow first side to brown. Turn over and finish browning. Serve with real New England maple syrup and whipped butter.

Lemon Mousse

7   eggs
4   yolks
8   Tbs. sugar
    rind of 4 lemons, *grated*
3   Tbs. gelatin
4   lemons, *juice of*
¼   cup heavy cream

Beat whites and cream. Soften gelatin with water. Beat yolks and sugar until fluffy. Add juice and rind. Heat gelatin to dissolve. Fold into egg mixture. Fold in cream and let it set in the refrigerator.

Place 4 oz. of mousse in hazelnut twill, garnish with fresh whipped cream and mint. Drizzle with fresh raspberry sauce.

W HETHER you spend a whole week or just a day, the surreal memories of Shelter Harbor Inn will last for years to come. This inn of Westerly, Rhode Island is committed to unpretentious furnishings and old-time cheer as evidenced throughout the estate: in a comfortable guest room that used to be a barn, in a cozy library that once was the living room of an old farmhouse.

The main house has ten guest rooms, each with a private bath and some with fireplaces and decks. A small carriage house has four additional guest rooms, each with access to a deck that offers a sweeping view of Block Island.

The decidedly laid-back atmosphere is ideal for vacationing families or groups seeking a mixture of business and pleasure. Spend a leisurely afternoon in a spirited game of croquet on the inn's well-groomed court. Or take in the sights at the famous Mystic Seaport, known the world over for its maritime museum and Mystic Marine-life Aquarium, both just minutes away. A daytime excursion to Block Island by way of its ferry is a pleasant alternative to seeing the sights by car. Watersports enthusiasts will revel in the opportunities for fishing, boating and swimming in nearby waters. Shelter Harbor Inn even has its own two-mile stretch of beach along Quonochontaug Pond and the ocean.

Lucky for New Englanders and those who travel here, the water is more than a place to set sail or catch a wave. It is the cherished source for the region's noted seafood specialties. At the Shelter Harbor Inn, the chef brings to the table a bounty of fresh seafood from the waters of Block Island Sound. Of course, all the foods traditional to New England are served as well, including Rhode Island Johnny Cakes, spread with whipped butter and real maple syrup. With an exquisite selection of vintage wines on hand, the server will be happy to suggest the perfect accompaniment to the meal.

Hazelnut Chicken with Orange Thyme Cream

1	large orange
1	whole boneless breast of chicken, *skinned and halved*
$\frac{1}{3}$	cup husked hazelnuts, *finely chopped*
$\frac{1}{3}$	cup fresh bread crumbs
$\frac{1}{4}$	tsp. dried thyme, *crumbled*
	all purpose flour
1	egg, *beaten to blend with 1 Tbs. water*
3	Tbs. unsalted butter
1	cup heavy cream
$\frac{1}{2}$	cup fresh orange juice
1	Tbs. frangelico liqueur
$\frac{1}{8}$	tsp. dried thyme, *crumbled*
	salt
	pepper, *freshly ground*

Remove peel and white pith from orange. Cut between membrane with small sharp knife to release orange segments. Using a flat mallet or rolling pin, pound chicken between 2 sheets of waxed paper to thickness of $\frac{1}{2}$". Combine hazelnuts, bread crumbs and $\frac{1}{4}$ tsp. thyme on large plate. Dredge chicken in flour, shaking off excess. Dip into egg, then into hazelnut mixture, shaking off excess. Melt butter in heavy skillet over medium heat. Add chicken and cook until golden brown and springy to the touch, about 3 minutes per side. Transfer to plates. Tent with foil to keep warm. Stir cream, orange juice, liqueur and $\frac{1}{8}$ tsp. thyme into skillet and bring to a boil. Reduce heat and simmer until reduced to $\frac{2}{3}$ cup. Season with salt and pepper. Add orange sections. Spoon sauce over chicken and serve.

Chicken Barley Soup
Serves 12

$\frac{3}{4}$	cup barley, *soaked*
1	gallon strong chicken stock
6	($\frac{1}{2}$) chicken breasts, *cooked and diced*
2	medium onions, *diced*
3	carrots, *diced*
4	stalks of celery
2	ea. zucchini, *diced*
2	ea. summer squash, *diced*
2	ea. leeks, *sliced*
2	ea. red bell peppers, *diced*
1	bay leaf
	salt and pepper, *to taste*
	fresh parsley
	garlic, *minced*
	herbs

Soak barley in water over night. Drain. Sauté all vegetables in a large stock pot until tender. Add spices and barley. Cover with stock and simmer until done (approximately 30 minutes). Remove bay leaf and garnish with chicken.

The Dorset Inn

DORSET, VERMONT
Chocolate Terrine

6 oz. unsalted butter
13 oz. semi-sweet chocolate chips
Melt.

10 egg yolks plus 4 Tbs. sugar
Beat.

¾ cup whipping cream
Whip.

Then add:
2 egg whites and a pinch of salt
Whip.

Then fold in:
1 Tbs. sugar

Freeze before glazing. Use ganache for glaze.

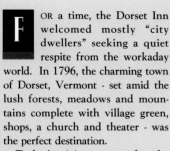

F OR a time, the Dorset Inn welcomed mostly "city dwellers" seeking a quiet respite from the workaday world. In 1796, the charming town of Dorset, Vermont - set amid the lush forests, meadows and mountains complete with village green, shops, a church and theater - was the perfect destination.

Today's visitors come for the same reasons. They come from all areas, be it big city, middle suburbia or small rural town.

Its recent restoration resulted in a marvelous mixture of old colonial style and modern convenience. Wide pine board floors, well-appointed furnishings and period architecture attest to the inn's historical character.

The innkeepers have a passion for fine food, as one is the inn's head chef - and a highly acclaimed one at that. Sumptuous flavors and artful presentation are the rewards of her skillful hand. Be assured, the meals are truly delightful at the Dorset Inn.

Yam Fritters
Serves 4

2   lbs. yams, *boiled until just soft but firm enough to be grated*

Mix together:

1   Tbs. flour
$\frac{1}{2}$ tsp. baking powder
$\frac{1}{2}$ tsp. salt
$\frac{1}{2}$ tsp. cinnamon
$\frac{1}{2}$ tsp. nutmeg
1   egg

Mix above with grated yams, make into balls. Roll in flour. Deep fry at 350 degrees in oil until brown (approximately 4 minutes).

Pear and Cider Cream Breast of Chicken
Serves 2

2   chicken breasts
2   medium pears, *peeled*
2   cups apple cider
3   Tbs. butter
2   Tbs. applejack brandy
    seasoned flour
    salt and pepper

Bone and skin 2 chicken breasts. Coat with seasoned flour, then sauté over low heat in 1 Tbs. of butter. Poach 2 pears in a sauce pan with apple cider for 10 minutes. Slice 1 poached pear for garnish, dice the other for the sauce. When chicken is browned on both sides, set it aside on a warm plate. Deglaze the pan over a high flame with 2 Tbs. of applejack, burning off the liquor. Add the cider in which the pears were poached and bring to a boil. Reduce heat, simmer for 1 minute and thicken to a cornstarch consistency. Whisk in 2 Tbs. of butter, adding salt and pepper if desired. Stir the diced pear into the sauce just before serving. Place the chicken breast on a warm plate, pour the sauce over the breasts and garnish with sliced pears.

YORK, Me.

Lobster Dublin Lawyer
Serves 2

1	2-lb. lobster
8	oz. sea scallops
6	tsp. butter
1	shallot, *minced*
2	Tbs. garlic butter
¼	cup heavy cream
¼	cup white wine

Cook lobster in boiling water for 5 minutes, split, remove meat and reserve the body. Heat butter in a heavy pan until frothy, add shallots and scallops. Sauté a few minutes then steam briefly with a splash of wine. Add lobster meat and heat thoroughly. Add whiskey, let it warm for a moment and ignite. When flames die down, add heavy cream and reduce, do not boil. Finish sauce garlic butter. To serve, place reserved body cavity on heated plate with boiled rice. Place scallops and lobster in shell, cover with sauce.

Apple Crisp

5	cups apples, *peeled and sliced*
⅓	cup water
¾	cup flour
1	cup sugar
½	tsp. cinnamon
¼	tsp. salt
¼	lb. butter, *cut in small pieces*

Preheat oven to 350 degrees. Butter a 1¼ quart baking dish. Spread apples in the dish and sprinkle the water on top. Combine the flour, sugar, cinnamon and salt in a bowl and rub in the butter with your fingers until it resembles coarse crumbs. Spread evenly over the apples. Bake for about 30 minutes or until crust is browned. Serve with vanilla ice cream.

Key Lime Pie

4	egg yolks
½	cup key lime juice
1	small can sweetened condensed milk
1	tsp. vanilla

Beat egg yolks until pale yellow and ribbon-like. Slowly add condensed milk. Beat until blended. Slowly add key lime juice. Add 1 tsp. of vanilla. Pour into a graham cracker crust. Bake at 350 degrees for 10 minutes. Top with freshly whipped cream. Garnish with fresh lime.

DOCKSIDE Guest Quarters, with its casual style and informal surroundings, is among Maine's most enjoyable inns. It's a place where families come together. Young and old, guests are never wanting for places to go or things to do.

Nestled in its own peninsula, the family-run lodge is situated on Harris Island, across the harbor of York, Maine. The Maine House and four cozy cottages overlook the gleaming York Harbor and the mighty Atlantic. With a full-service marina, sandy beaches and fishing charters, the area is a virtual water wonderland.

A flurry of nautical activity takes place at Dockside, from whale watching and lobstering excursions, to harbor tours and riverboat cruises. Anglers delight in the incredible variety of fish - striped sea bass, bluefish and giant tuna - reeled in from deep sea excursions. Even casting a line from the pier yields a plentiful catch of flounder.

The hard-packed beaches of Short Sands and Long Sands find grown-ups and children busy at play. Some build sandcastles, while others settle in and soak up the sun.

Venture over to colonial York Village for a firsthand look at America's first chartered city. A leisurely tour of the Historic District brings to light a wealth of fascinating information. Among the registered sites are the Elizabeth Perkins House (1731), with its exquisite Victorian furnishings, and the John Hancock Warehouse, formerly owned by the illustrious signer of the Constitution.

Indeed, one of the highlights of vacationing is sampling the region's specialty foods. The Restaurant-at-Dockside does a fine job of preparing succulent Maine lobster and other ocean delicacies on its lunch and dinner menu. A continental breakfast featuring freshly-baked breads and muffins and just-picked fruits is served in the resort's Maine House.

Chatham Bars Inn

Chatham, MA.

Medallions of Veal Tenderloin with Ragout of Wild Mushrooms and Fingerling Potatoes
Serves 5

Mushroom Ragout:

8	oz. shiitake mushrooms
8	oz. criminis mushrooms
8	oz. oyster mushrooms
8	oz. potabelos
4	oz. shallots
4	oz. fingerling potatoes

Blanch mushrooms and allow to cool, drain. Reserve juices, refrigerate mushrooms until needed. Cook potatoes and peel, cool and slice approximately $\frac{1}{4}$" thick. Slice shallots, caramelize with butter. Brown potatoes in the same pan, add back shallots and mushrooms. Season to taste, sauté until mushrooms are hot. Reserve.

Sauce:

$\frac{1}{2}$	cup shallots, *small diced*
750 L.	madeira wine
$\frac{1}{2}$	cup veal demi-glace
	salt and white pepper, *to taste*
2	Tbs. butter

Caramelize shallots. Add madeira, reduce 2-3 times. Add demi-glace and juice from mushrooms. Reduce until thick, whisk in butter. Season to taste. Strain, keep warm.

5	ea. $2\frac{3}{4}$ oz. medallions of tenderloins
2	oz. olive oil
10	ea. large shallots
2	cups red wine
	salt and pepper, *to taste*

Slice shallots thin, cover with red wine. Cook until all wine is absorbed. Add remaining wine, repeat process. Keep warm until needed. Sauté veal medallions. Place mushroom ragout at top of plate and veal medallions on bottom of plate with shallot comfit. Ladle sauce around veal.

Nauset Blue Mussels and Champagne Soup
Serves 5

30	ea. Nauset blue mussels
4	oz. shallots
1	Tbs. garlic cloves, *crushed*
1	tsp. whole white peppercorns
6	ea. parsley stems
1	bay leaf
1	qt. champagne
1	qt. heavy cream
5	oz. creme fraiche
	salt, white pepper and cayenne pepper, *to taste*

Wash mussels well, remove beards. Place in sauce pot with sliced shallots, garlic, peppercorns, stems, bay leaf and champagne. Cover and cook until the mussels fully open. Remove mussels from pot, allow to cool. Remove them from shells and refrigerate until needed. Reduce champagne by half, being careful not to brown side of pot. Add heavy cream and allow to reduce to desired consistency. Strain the soup and whisk in the creme fraiche, season to taste. Keep hot until needed. Heat mussels and serve with soup in soup plates. Garnish with chervil.

Medallions of Beef Tenderloin with Salad of Brussels Sprouts, Turnip and Morels
Serves 5

2	lb. beef tenderloin cut into 10 ea. $3\frac{1}{4}$-$3\frac{1}{2}$ oz. medallions
6	oz. brussels sprout leaves
8	oz. turnip
8	oz. morels
2	sprigs of thyme
2	Tbs. garlic, *minced*
2	oz. white wine vinegar
10	oz. balsamic vinegar sauce

Soak the morels in water and vinegar. Cut and sauté in olive oil. Julienne the turnip and blanch in salted water. Clean brussels sprout leaves and blanch. Mix all the vegetables in mixing bowl with minced shallots, garlic, thyme and chives. Add vinegar and season with salt, pepper, nutmeg and sugar. Heat sauté pan with olive oil and sauté the seasoned beef to desired doneness. Let rest. Serve salad and beef with balsamic vinegar sauce.

Monkfish Dusted in Cloves with Pancetta, Upland Cress, Potato and Truffle homefries
Serves 4

Shallot Purée:

6	oz. shallots
2	cups vermouth
$\frac{1}{2}$	lemon, *juice of*
$\frac{1}{2}$	cup creme fraiche
	salt and pepper, *to taste*
	cayenne pepper, *to taste*
	lemon juice, *to taste*

Bring shallots, vermouth and lemon to a boil. Simmer until shallots are very tender. Strain and reserve liquid. Place shallots in blender with creme fraiche, purée. Season to taste and keep warm.

P ERHAPS only a handful of inns offers traditional clam and lobster bakes right on the water's edge. For this reason, and many more as one soon discovers, the Chatham Bars Inn is one of America's premier ocean-front resorts.

Guests come to this Cape Cod landmark to rest and rejuvenate. The inn's theme and holiday weekends are big hits, too. Music and dancing (Last Tango in Chatham Weekend), vintner and culinary galas (Viva Italia! Weekend) and murder mysteries (Murder by the Sea Weekend) give a hint to the intriguing festivities planned year-round.

Secluded beaches, exciting seafaring adventures, exquisite shopping, fascinating historical tours...pick and choose, or choose them all.

An award-winning chef prepares the outstanding cuisine of Chatham Inn. All the treats of the sea - Atlantic salmon and halibut, Nantucket scallops, Yellowfin tuna and Blue mussels - are skillfully prepared and presented in gracious New England style.

Monkfish

2½	lbs. monkfish
	tempura flour, *as needed*
	ground cloves, *to taste*
2	oz. olive oil
4½	oz. whole butter
2	oz. pancetta, *sliced thinly*
12	ea. white potatoes
	cooked, peeled and sliced
2	Tbs. truffle breakings
2	bunches upland cress
	salt, pepper, nutmeg and madeira sauce, *to taste*

Mix tempura flour and ground cloves. Season monkfish, lightly coat with flour. Heat olive oil in sauté pan. Place monkfish in pan to roast. Add the whole butter. Once monkfish is seared, slow heat and continually baste monkfish with the butter and juices. Meanwhile, sauté potato slices with whole butter until starting to turn golden brown. Add truffles, continue to cook until golden brown. Season to taste, add fresh marjoram. Cut monkfish in half, arrange on warm plates with shallot purée. Quickly cook pancetta slices, arrange on top of monkfish with cress. Drizzle madeira sauce on cress and around fish. Arrange potato and truffles on plate and serve.

Warm Chocolate Cake with Vanilla Ice Cream
Serves 6

5½	oz. bittersweet chocolate
5½	oz. whole butter
3	ea. whole eggs
3	ea. egg yolks
3	oz. sugar
2½	oz. all purpose flour

Melt chocolate and butter together and set aside. Combine eggs, yolks, and sugar and beat for 10 minutes or until light in color and thick. Gradually add sifted flour and continue to mix until thoroughly combined. Pour into buttered and floured molds and bake for 9 to 12 minutes at 325 degrees. Center should be soft and slightly unset. Serve immediately dusted with confectionery sugar and topped with chocolate curls. Place quenelles of vanilla ice cream next to cake.

Yankee Clipper Inn

Rockport, MA.

Lobster Polenta with
Boursin Cheese Sauce
Serves 6-8

Lobster Polenta:

4½	cups water
1	Tbs. salt
3	Tbs. olive oil
½	cup shallots, *diced*
6	cloves of garlic, *crushed*
¼	cup scallions, *diced*
1	tsp. dried basil
1	tsp. dried oregano
10	ounces lobster meat, *cooked and diced*
1½	cups corn meal

In a heavy sauce pot, bring water and salt to a boil. In a separate skillet, heat olive oil on medium heat, add shallots, garlic, scallions and herbs, sauté until shallots are soft, add lobster and mix well. When water is boiling, add lobster mixture. Bring back to a boil then gradually add corn meal, stirring continually to avoid lumps. Reduce heat to low and continue to stir, cook for 15 minutes. The polenta is done when it comes cleanly away from the sides of the pot. Place the polenta in a lightly greased 5" x 9" loaf pan to cool.

Baked Stuffed Lobster
Verandah
Serves 2

Preheat oven to 375 degrees.

2	1½-1¼ pound lobsters, *live and active*
12	cups of water
1	Tbs. salt
1	cup white cream sauce
1	cup sea scallops
1	cup mushrooms, *sliced*
¼	cup scallions, *diced*
2	shallots, *diced*
1	Tbs. butter
1	Tbs. white wine
1	tsp. dry sherry
½	cup Italian season bread crumbs
2	Tbs. parmesan cheese, *grated*

White Sauce:

2	Tbs. butter
2	Tbs. all purpose flour

¼	tsp. salt
¼	tsp. dried marjoram
¼	tsp. dried basil
	dash of pepper
1	cup half and half

In small sauce pan, melt butter. Stir in flour and seasoning, mix and cook for 2 minutes, add half and half. Cook and stir over medium heat until thickened. Cook and stir 1 to 2 minutes more. Set aside.

Cooking Lobsters:
In a large kettle, combine water and salt. Bring to a boil. Plunge the lobsters into the water, return to a boil, cook until the lobsters have turned red then remove and let cool to touch. Placing lobsters on their backs, cut lobsters in half lengthwise up to the tail section, leaving shell back intact, remove tail meat.

Lobster Stuffing:
In a sauté skillet, melt the butter on medium heat, add the lobster tail meat cut lengthwise in two, scallops, mushrooms and scallions and shallots. Sauté until scallops are firm, add white wine and mix well, lower heat. Combine white sauce and sherry with the lobster/scallop mixture, stirring to combine and heat sauce through. Add bread crumbs, stir to combine.

Stuffing the Lobster:
Place the lobsters on a baking dish, backs down and folded open. Divide the stuffing between the lobsters, placing the mixture into the cavity of the lobster, sprinkle the parmesan cheese then bake for 15 minutes. Remove from oven and serve.

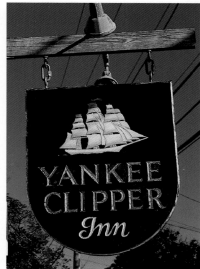

ITTING on the veranda, sipping afternoon tea, it just doesn't get any better than this. The attentive and cordial staff at the Yankee Clipper Inn goes to great lengths to ensure a pleasurable visit. From the innovative New England cuisine, to arranging sightseeing tours, the comfort and pleasure of its guests are top priority.

The Inn offers oceanfront lodging, just off the ruggedly beautiful Rockport shoreline, with each guest room named for a famous nineteenth century New England clipper ship. The property also includes two additional guest houses. The Bulfinch House, an 1840 Greek Revival, was designed by distinguished architect, John Bulfinch. The more contemporary Quarterdeck, built in 1960, features oversized windows for enjoying panoramic views of the deep blue sea.

Apple Crumb Pie

Filling:
10 apples
¼ cup all purpose flour
½ cup brown sugar
½ tsp. nutmeg
½ tsp. cinnamon

Topping:
1½ cup brown sugar
1½ cup quick cooking oats
1 cup all purpose flour
¾ cup butter, *melted*

Line 9" pie pan with single layer pie crust. Preheat oven to 350 degrees. Peel and slice apples, combine with flour, brown sugar, nutmeg and cinnamon. Mix well coating apples, place in pie shell. Combine brown sugar, oats, flour and cinnamon, mix. Cut in butter, mixing into a coarse crumb mixture. Place on top of pie, patting in place. Bake for 20 to 25 minutes or until crust is golden brown. Serve warm with vanilla ice cream.

Red Pepper Jelly

¾ cup red peppers (*approx. 3*)
1 Tbs. cayenne pepper
6 cups sugar
1½ cups cider vinegar
1 package Certo fruit pectin (*liquid*)

Clean and slice peppers, place in a food processor and purée with half the vinegar and cayenne pepper. Pour into a sauce pan with the rest of the vinegar and sugar. Bring to a boil, stirring constantly and boil for 5 minutes. Remove from heat, cool for 2 minutes, add pectin and stir well. Let cool. Serve with whipped cream cheese and crackers.

Boursin Cheese Sauce

½ cup half and half cream
5.2 oz package of Boursin Cheese

In the top of a double boiler, heat the cheese and cream until smooth and warm. In a skillet over medium high heat, heat enough olive oil to coat the bottom of the skillet. Slice the polenta across the loaf, sauté each slice until golden on both sides. Place polenta slices on a tray and pour warm sauce over them. Garnish with parsley and lemon.

The Mayflower Inn

Washington, Ct.

Garlic and Rosemary Roasted Rack of Pork with Apple Pear Sauce

1   ea. rack of pork
    *bones frenched, chine bone removed
    and reserved olive oil as needed*
1   cup onions, *diced*
1   cup celery, *diced*
1   cup carrots, *diced*
1   cup leeks, *diced*
12 ea. garlic cloves, *peeled*
2   Tbs. rosemary leaves
1   qt. chicken stock
    salt and pepper, *as needed*

Lightly oil rack of pork, crush garlic cloves and rub vigorously around meat. Season with rosemary leaves, salt and pepper. In roasting pan, place reserved chine bone, put pork rack on top, surround these with diced vegetables. Roast in preheated 450 degree oven for 20 minutes, reduce heat to 325 degrees, continue to cook for 30 minutes more until meat thermometer registers 140 degrees. Remove pork from pan and keep warm. Place roasting pan on top of stove and add chicken stock, scraping from bottom of pan to loosen meat drippings. Reduce by half. Strain and degrease. Adjust seasonings. Slice pork rack between bones and pass pork jus and apple pear sauce separately.

Garlic Cream

12 ea. garlic cloves, *unpeeled*
    vegetable oil, *as needed*
1   cup heavy cream

Lightly oil garlic cloves, roast in a 350 degree oven for 15 minutes or until tender. Peel garlic when cool enough to handle. Put garlic and cream in sauce pan, bring to a boil, then purée in blender. Refrigerate until ready to use.

Warm Semolina Terrine with Quince Sauce and Creme Fraiche

Serves 6

Semolina Terrine:
1   qt. milk
1   vanilla bean
4   oz. sugar
6   oz. semolina
3   ea. whole eggs
2   ea. egg yolks
2   oz. butter

Bring milk to a boil with the sugar and the split and scraped vanilla bean. Slowly add semolina and cook at low heat for 10 minutes. Remove from stove and add eggs, egg yolks and butter. Line a 2 quart terrine mold with plastic wrap. Put semolina mixture in the terrine and enclose with overhanging plastic. Cover top with aluminum foil. Place in a water bath and bake in a 350 degree oven for 1 hour. Cool, then refrigerate until ready to use.

Quince Sauce:
4   ea. ripe quince
    washed, quartered and seeds removed
1   qt. water
4   cups sugar
3   ea. vanilla beans, *split*
1   fresh bay leaf

Bring water to boil, add the scrapings from the 3 split vanilla beans. Add the sugar and bay leaf, bring to a boil and cook for 2 minutes. Add quince quarters, lower temperature and cook until tender. Remove bay leaf and when cool, purée in a blender. Hold for service.

To Serve: Remove semolina terrine from mold and unwrap. Cut 6 pieces ¾" thick. Place on cookie sheet, sprinkle with sugar, brown under broiler. Place 4 ounces of quince sauce in middle of each dessert plate, top with slice of terrine. Place a heaping tablespoon of creme fraiche on bottom left hand corner of terrine. Garnish with a mint sprig and serve.

IN the spirit of a grand European country home, the Mayflower Inn is every bit as splendid. Gloriously appointed - top to bottom, inside and out. No detail is too fine. From the eighteenth century Chippendale desk, complete with stationery, to the country-fragrant shampoos, body lotions and conditioners furnished in the spacious marble baths, the Mayflower Inn is very much a place "where comfort meets connoisseurship."

The innkeepers, with their refined sense of style and decorative talents, have furnished the estate's three buildings - Mayflower, Speedwell and Standish - with exquisite antiques, art and collectibles from England, France and America. Tabriz rugs. Frette linens. Down comforters. White Limoges china. All the warm, inviting pleasures of a home away from one's own are generously provided.

Each of the 24 guest rooms is individually appointed with romantic four-poster canopied antique beds, plump pillows and fine linens. Luxurious baths with vanities of shiny brass and rich mahogany have oversized tubs ideal for a long soak, a sip of champagne or a quiet read.

As one might expect, the dining services at the Mayflower Inn leave nothing to be desired. Sumptuous dishes prepared with fresh organic herbs and produce (from the local garden, of course), choice meats and fish and scratch breads and pastries round out a diverse and ever-changing menu. Thanks to a chef of exacting skill and willful creativity, the restaurant enjoys four-star praises from some of the area's most discriminating critics.

Vegetable Stock

2½	qts. water
½	cup onion, *chopped*
½	cup leek, *chopped*
¼	cup carrots, *chopped*
¼	cup celery, *chopped*
½	cup tomato, *chopped*
¼	cup parsnip, *chopped*
½	cup mushrooms, *chopped*
	vegetable oil, *as needed*
3	ea. garlic cloves, *crushed*

Heat vegetable oil in stock pot, add vegetables and cook for 3 to 5 minutes. Add water, bring to a boil and cook for 1 hour. Strain, cool and refrigerate until needed.

Butternut Squash Soup with Roasted Garlic Cream

2	ea. butternut squash, *peeled, seeded and diced*
2	qts. vegetable stock (*recipe above*)
1	cup garlic cream (*recipe on opposite page*)
	chives, *minced (as needed)*

Bring vegetable stock to a boil. Add squash, cook until tender. Cool, then purée in blender. Check seasonings with salt and pepper. Whip garlic cream, check seasonings with salt and pepper. Reheat soup, place 6 ounces in soup bowl. Garnish with 2 Tbs. of whipped garlic cream and minced chives.

Apple Pear Sauce

6	ea. red apples (*McIntosh, Red Delicious*), *quartered, seeded*
6	ea. Bartlett pears, *peeled, quartered and seeded*
2	ea. lemons, juice of
½	tsp. cinnamon
	pinch of salt
½	cup brown sugar
¼	tsp. nutmeg
1	bay leaf

Put all ingredients in a heavy duty sauce pan with 1 ounce of water, and cover. Cook over medium heat, stirring occasionally until apples and pears have completely broken down (about 25 minutes). Remove from stove and pass through a fine strainer. Check seasoning and sweetness to taste. Allow to cool before using.

The Mayflower Inn